# Innovative Marketing Strategies

# Table of Contents

# Chapter 1 – How and Why Creative Marketing Works

Today's business market is an extremely competitive place. More businesses enter the fray all the time: for the past ten years, more than 750,000 new startups spring into existence across North America. Unfortunately, over 60 percent of new businesses fail in the first four years.

Why do they fail? According to a study performed by the U.S. Department of Commerce, there are three main reasons startup businesses fold:

- Lack of financial planning
- Poor sales skills
- Poorly planned and executed marketing

Creative marketing addresses all three of these concerns. It is one of the most successful marketing methods available, and since it is low-cost and high-impact, you won't need a huge advertising budget to take advantage of this powerful strategy.

What you will need is a basic understanding of how and why Creative marketing works.

## *The Element of Surprise*

One of the reasons Creative marketing works is that the methods are often unexpected. Many Creative campaigns are highly visible, and contain some sort of element that is unique to the business using it.

Though it is something of a cliché by now, you should be prepared to "think outside the box" when it comes to planning your Creative marketing campaign. The classic, expensive methods of advertising your business should be employed sparingly, if at all. These include:

- Yellow page advertisements
- Newspaper or magazine advertisements
- Radio or television commercials

Think about it: when is the last time you were heavily influenced by a yellow page, newspaper, magazine, radio, or television advertisement? The fact is that today's consumers are so bombarded with advertising messages, they've learned to tune out the traditional sources.

As a Creative marketer, your goal is to catch them off-guard, and advertise in unexpected places. Many times, consumers won't even recognize your marketing efforts as advertising.

The good news is: you can usually do this for a fraction of the cost of traditional advertising venues. Creative marketing trades effort for money. You will work harder on your marketing than a mega-corporation with a million-dollar ad budget, but if you are persistent and creative in your efforts, they will pay off.

## *It Pays to Be Different*

Remember the old Arby's slogan: "Different is Good"? This catchy little phrase could serve as a basic premise for one of the primary reasons Creative marketing tactics are so successful.

You might have a product or service that is completely unique. However, the chances are greater that you're competing with dozens or hundreds of other businesses for the same market share. One of the strengths of Creative marketing is the ability to capitalize on the aspect or aspects of your business that make you different -- and therefore worthy enough for consumers to spend their hard-earned money on your product or service.

So, what's different about your business? Here is a brief list of possibilities to investigate. Your business might offer:

- The best, friendliest, or most attentive customer service.
- The lowest prices.
- Products that are higher quality than the competition.
- A wider range of products than other businesses in your area or field.
- The simplest ordering methods.
- Fast, convenient, and/or reliable delivery.
- More expertise in your area than your competition.
- The most informative and easiest to navigate website.

This aspect of your business is sometimes referred to as your USP, or Unique Selling Proposition. Once you have determined your USP, you know what makes your business different -- and different is good!

### *Controls and Variables*

As with any marketing campaign, there are a lot of different variables that concern the outcome of your Creative marketing efforts. Some have to do with your business, which is often largely in your control. Others have to do with your customers, which are not always under your control.

When it comes to your business, the variables you will have to consider during the planning stage of your marketing campaign include:

- Your location: If you run a brick-and-mortar business, where will your customers come from? Is there a decent amount of walk-in traffic, or are you situated out of the way? If you work from home or online, is your website at a good "location" - meaning well ranked with search engines, and parked at a domain that is easy for people to remember or stumble across?
- Your product or service: The specific tangible and intangible items offered by your business will play a large role in determining how you'll market yourself.
- Your target market: What is the best way to reach people who are most likely to become your customers? Identifying and reaching your target market is covered more extensively in chapter 3 of this book.
- Your attitude: Though this is not an aspect that is specific to your business, it is one that you can control. If you remain positive and upbeat in your approach to business, your marketing efforts will reflect that attitude -- and your customers will notice.

What about your customers? Other people's reactions are for the most part beyond your control. You may have the best sales pitch and the most compelling marketing campaign out there, but potential customers who happen to be having a bad day when they see your message aren't likely to react in your favor.

However, there are some things you can control in regard to your customers. One of these things is to understand why people buy -- what brings them from initial interest to final sale. There are many different reasons, so you should determine which of them might apply to your business and focus on them.

To name just a few, consumers buy products or services that will:

- Make them money (turnkey or reseller programs are a good example of this).
- Get them praise (gifts, new clothing).

- Keep up with the Joneses (when "everyone else" has something).
- Make them look younger, better, or smarter.
- Possess beautiful objects or works of art.
- Make them more comfortable.
- Be more efficient, either at work or at home.
- Make their work easier or faster.
- Help them avoid hard work.
- Protect their family or their possessions.
- Excite or entertain them.
- Inform them or enrich their lives.
- Allow them to escape stress.
- Boost their popularity or reputation.
- Save them money or time.
- Help them express emotions to others.
- Satisfy their curiosity.
- Attract the opposite sex.
- Help them avoid missing an opportunity.

It is important to become familiar with the needs your business fulfills for your customers. Armed with this knowledge, you can build a marketing campaign that points out the benefits consumers will realize when they purchase your product or service.

### Fun with Case Studies

Does Creative marketing really work? Since the widespread embrace of the concept, many companies have undertaken successful Creative marketing campaigns. Innovation is often the key to a thriving business, and the following companies are examples of Creative effectiveness in action.

## Several Campaigns That Worked

*Saint Paul, Minnesota:* Before the opening of the first Crazy Carrot Juice Bar, marketer Eric Strauss engaged in some forward thinking. He spent $73 to put together a life-sized carrot costume, which was worn at several special events around town.

Over the next year, the "Carrot" made many public appearances. It was featured in various print, radio, and television media, and became largely responsible for catapulting the company's success. Eventually, the Crazy Carrot Juice Bar expanded to five stores and 65 employees, and was then sold to industry giant Jamba Juice -- all for a mere $73 investment.

*Irvington, New York:* The Flying Fingers Yarn Shop, just outside of Manhattan, was looking to expand its customer base. At the suggestion of a marketing consultant, the company secured three giant balls of yarn, complete with knitting needles, to the roof of a modified van and called it the Yarn Bus.

On weekends, the Yarn Bus travels between Irvington and NYC, promoting visibility and making special appearances at news events. Flying Fingers has seen a good increase in store traffic, but more importantly, people who might not make the physical trip to the store are made aware of their website, where they can learn about knitting classes offered by the store and purchase knitting supplies. The high visibility of the Yarn Bus has produced excellent results.

*Manhattan, New York:* Even not-for-profit businesses look to expand their reach. The Marble Church sought a way to attract younger members and revitalize their congregation. So, they turned to a marketing firm who came up with some unusual ways to get the word out.

One Labor Day weekend, hundreds of  weekend visitors to the Hamptons spotted an airplane banner bearing the intriguing message: "Make a friend in a very high place.

Marblechurch.org." In addition, the church rented a low-cost mobile billboard (mounted on the side of a van) that drove around Manhattan. The sign read: "In This Town It Doesn't Hurt to Have God on Your Side."

These creative messages, delivered in creative ways, introduced Marble Church to people who would otherwise never have heard of the place. As a result, the church reported a 31% increase in membership.

*Oregon:* Odd giveaways abound. People are intrigued by the unusual, which may explain why the Les Schwab tire dealership's "free beef in February" promotion keeps customers coming back, or why a nearby bank receives excellent local media coverage for their yearly tradition of giving away free Vidalia onions to anyone who walks in.

## One Campaign That Didn't

Remember the backfiring efforts mentioned in the first chapter?

Recently, a Creative marketing campaign took a surprisingly bad turn in Boston, Massachusetts. In an effort to promote a new animated television series, *Aqua Teen Hunger Force*, the Cartoon Network designed and installed 40 magnetic light displays depicting characters from the series, and mounted them in various locations in and around Boston.

Unfortunately, Boston citizens reacted with suspicion to the devices, which included batteries and wires hooked to the back of the placards to control the lights. Reports of the signs caused a city-wide panic in post-9/11 fashion, and "an army of emergency vehicles" responded to the situation. Several bridges, subway stations and highways were closed while police examined and in some cases destroyed the signs.

What marketing impact did this incident have for Cartoon Network? It certainly raised awareness of the program, but when it comes to your business, you may not want this level of advertising. TV columnist David Hiltbrand stated for the *Philadelphia Inquirer*: "Those wacky marketing guys at Turner Broadcasting. Because, let's face it, nothing says cartoon hijinks quite like a red-level terrorist threat."

# Chapter 2 – Creative Marketing for Your Small Business

In this chapter, we'll start with a closer look at what Creative marketing entails, and then discuss some of the groundwork you should be doing before you plan and execute your campaign.

Unlike other marketing methods, which rely on a huge influx of cash and resources designed to bring about immediate results, Creative marketing takes time and continual effort to sustain. In any marketing venture, it can be difficult to gauge the effectiveness of a particular technique. When it comes to Creative marketing, you will notice results that are a culmination of many different areas.

Let me introduce you to Jay Conrad Levinson from http://www.gmarketing.com According to the father of the intense 'out of the box' Guerrilla marketing, the following basic principles lie at the heart of the Creative world:

- Though large corporations have used Jay's Guerrilla techniques with some success, the methods are best geared for small businesses.
- Creative marketing is based on principles of human psychology -- the study of the various ways consumers react to a marketing message -- rather than experience and guesswork.
- A combination of marketing methods is a must for Creative success -- do not rely on a single advertising venue
- Embracing current technology is of primary importance. Creative marketing is all about the cutting edge.
- You should plan to invest significant portions of time, energy, and creativity into your Creative marketing strategy, rather than money.
- Instead of sales volume, your business success should be measured in profits.
- Creative marketing campaigns concentrate on building new relationships with complementary businesses, rather than trying to beat out the competition.

- Shift your focus away from getting new customers; instead, aim for more, larger transactions with existing customers and more customer referrals (facilitating word of mouth, which is discussed in the next chapter).

Is Creative marketing right for your business? In most cases, the answer is yes.

## *Advantages*

We'll start with the good stuff:

- Creative marketing is cheap. At the high end, you may end up investing a few hundred dollars in promotional items or a major, centralized piece that you can build a number of different campaigns around (such as the  carrot suit in the examples listed in chapter 2). At the low end, it's free -- and you can't beat free!
- In addition to growing your business, Creative marketing involves networking, both with your customers and with other businesses. In the process of executing and maintaining your campaign, you will make a lot of new friends and allies.
- Creative marketing is specifically tailored to meet the needs of small businesses, whereas traditional advertising venues are complicated and expensive to the point of exclusion (bordering on snobbishness).
- Many aspects of Creative marketing campaigns are just plain fun! You get to perform wacky stunts and engage in unusual activities, all in the name of working for a living.
- Creative marketing works. If you do your research, plan your campaign, and stick with it, you will more than likely end up with a better and more profitable business.

## *Disadvantages*

And now, the bad:

- Creative marketing works -- but it is not completely failsafe. It is, after all, advertising; which is far from an exact science. The number of variables involved in advertising guarantees that nothing is 100 percent effective.

- As with any advertising campaign, you will not be able to pinpoint exactly what works and what doesn't. Obtaining measurable results is difficult (but not impossible, unlike other marketing techniques).

- Creative marketing requires a greater level of dedication and energy than traditional advertising venues, which often consist of throwing large amounts of money at other people to do the work for you.

- If you're looking for a quick fix, Creative marketing is not your solution. You will not see instant or overnight results stemming from your efforts. An investment of time is required in order to achieve your business sales goals.

- Creative marketing is not for the thin-skinned or faint of heart. At the very least, you will have a few detractors who find fault in your methods. At worst, you may be threatened with legal action (which is why it's so important to check your local laws before engaging in a Creative marketing campaign).

### *Cost Breakdown: Money versus Effort*

What is worth more: your money, or your time?

This is the trade-off involved in Creative marketing. You don't need a lot of money, but if you don't invest your time, your efforts will not pay off. The principles behind Creative marketing (listed in the beginning of this chapter) require planning, groundwork, and effort.

How can you tell whether it's worth the trade-off?

Here is a brief, hypothetical example.

One popular marketing method is to send out e-mail announcements in the form of a regular weekly or monthly newsletter. You could build a mailing list and create your own newsletter (the Creative method) or you could buy advertising space in another business's newsletter (the traditional method).

**If you choose to advertise in another newsletter:**

- You will spend somewhere between $100 and $1000 for premium space in a widely read newsletter (e-zine) with a big subscriber list. You may end up spending more for consecutive ads, since consumers typically need to see your message 3 to 7 times before they'll buy.
- You will spend a few to several hours researching e-zines, writing your advertisements or article, and contacting the e-zine owners in order to schedule your ad's appearances.
- You will typically see a conversion rate (number of people who read your advertisement compared to number of people who become your customers) of 2 to 5 percent - slightly higher than the conversion rate of a direct mail campaign. This rate typically goes up a few percentages with subsequent advertisements, depending on the effectiveness of your copy (the wording of your message).

**If you create your own newsletter or e-zine:**

- You will spend $0 to $100 (you may decide to invest in desktop publishing software, list management software or services, or an upgraded Internet service provider plan to handle additional web traffic).
- You will spend several hours to several months building your opt-in subscription base, through methods like sign-up boxes, refer-a-friend programs, e-zine directory listings, and word of mouth.
- You will realize the typical conversion rate at first (2 to 5 percent) - but you will never have to spend another penny for advertising, because you own the newsletter or e-zine. Your subscription base will continue to grow, and your sales resulting from your

newsletter will increase exponentially, rather than in the measured bursts you can expect from the "traditional" method.

One thing to be wary of when you're building an e-zine subscription base is buying bulk lists and using "free traffic" programs to bulk up your subscribers. Though this will give you some impressive numbers, the majority of these will either delete your e-mails unread, or unsubscribe as soon as they've met the requirements of whatever benefit they signed up for. The best results will come from a carefully targeted subscriber list that you have built yourself.

**Determining your money-versus-time factor**

How can you figure out whether the time you'll invest in a given Creative marketing campaign is worth the trade-off in advertising dollars -- assuming, of course, that you have a substantial advertising budget to begin with? (If you don't, no worries; you don't need one!)

You can get a rough estimate of your results by performing the following steps:

1. Determine a traditional advertising venue that most closely relates to your intended Creative marketing effort.
2. Estimate the total monetary cost of each method.
3. Estimate the total time investment involved with each method.
4. Assign a reasonable dollar value to each hour of your time you would invest ($15 an hour is a good average).
5. Add monetary costs and per-hour time costs to each method, arriving at two separate totals.
6. Calculate a projected profit resulting from each of the methods (don't forget to factor in the "snowball" effect gained from Creative marketing through repeat business and customer referrals - most traditional advertising venues are one-shot deals).
7. Subtract total cost from total profit.

This will give you a general idea. Usually, the Creative marketing campaign will end up looking like a much better deal.

## *Finding Your Target Market*

Before you attempt to sell your products or services, you need to know to whom you're selling them. Market research is an important step in any advertising campaign, and one that is unfortunately overlooked too often. Without a good handle on your target market, you will be wasting your time, effort and money.

The most effective marketing is designed to specifically reach the people who are most likely to buy your product or service. This is one reason why traditional advertising has such a low response rate. Just about everyone has access to television, radio, and print media like newspapers and phone books. Only a small percentage of those people will be in your target demographic.

There are two steps to target marketing, which is also referred to as niche marketing. The first is to define your target, and the second is to find ways to reach them. Once you have accomplished these steps, you can incorporate this information into a Creative marketing campaign that will give you the most bang for your buck (or more likely, your efforts).

### Identifying your niche

This step involves a close analysis of your business. Much like an investigative reporter, you need to determine the who, what, where, when, and why of your customer base. Ask yourself the following questions:

- Would your product or service appeal more to men, women, or both genders equally?

- What age range does your product or service appeal to? (Note: if your business sells products or services for children, parents are your target demographic).

- What is the range of income and education level of the people who may be interested in your product or service?

- Are they single? Married? With children? Retired?

- How will your customers use your products or services? Is there a potential for repeat business?

- Does your product or service fall into the category of needs (food, clothing, shelter) or wants (luxury items)?

- What makes your product or service unique (your USP -- discussed in Chapter 2)?

- Is your product an impulse buy (books, shoes, gourmet food) or an investment (cars, boats, computer hardware or software)?

- How are transactions for your product or service typically carried out -- online, mail order, or in person? Cash, check, or credit cards? A single payment, multiple payments, or monthly recurring fees?

- How do your potential customers typically become alerted to new products or services? Online, through public advertisements, from the news media, or some other method?

You may even want to develop a profile of your ideal customer (for example, 20-30 year old single college-educated females, or 40-50 year old married males with middle-class incomes) to help you pinpoint your target market.

**Locating your niche**

Once you have determined what type of customer you're looking for, you have to find where they hang out. Do they frequently eat at restaurants or go to movies? Would they be more likely to spend an afternoon at a shopping mall or a library? Are they frequent travelers, and would you be able to reach them at airports and bus or train terminals?

For online marketing, you can often find specific forums for your target demographic. Keep in mind that when you're marketing online, you have to build a rapport with online communities before you can start pitching your business. After all, you wouldn't walk into a complete stranger's house and shove your products in their faces demanding a purchase, would you?  This may sound like an extreme example, but when it comes to Internet protocol, this is exactly what people seem like when they drop into forums and immediately start posting advertisements and special deals.

Use the information you find about your target customers' buying habits to determine the best ways to focus your Creative marketing efforts.  If your customers like to eat out, consider striking an exchange with a local restaurant.  If they travel, think about bus billboards or materials you can hand out in terminals.

# Chapter 3 – Creative Marketing Methods

Now that you know what Creative marketing can do for your business, it's time to learn how to do it!  In this chapter, we'll explore some of the methods you can use to build buzz and grab your customers' interest.

Keep in mind that there are many different approaches to Creative marketing, and your strategy should include some elements that are unique to your business. You don't have to follow these methods to the letter -- in fact, experimentation is a great way to hit on that perfect marketing strategy that will deliver the gold for you.  Feel free to tweak these methods and create an approach that is uniquely yours.

## *Word of Mouth*

Word of mouth marketing is arguably the most powerful and effective strategy out there. Unfortunately, it is also the most elusive and difficult to control.  This marketing method relies more on your customers than on your efforts, and can usually be traced to the quality of your product or service.

To put it another way: word of mouth marketing happens when a product or service "sells itself."

### What is it?

People like to talk. Word of mouth marketing, basically, is giving them something to talk about: your business. It is building a "buzz" about your product or service, and letting your customers do the marketing legwork for you by telling friends, family, and sometimes even complete strangers if they're excited enough.

Word of mouth marketing is powerful, because it is genuine.  You can't fake this phenomenon. When people believe what you have is worth mentioning to others, they're going to be enthusiastic -- and that enthusiasm helps to generate even more business for you in the form of new customers and wider market recognition.

There are many different forms word of mouth marketing can take. Just a few of them are:

- **Viral marketing:** Crafting and distributing a high-impact message that it easy to pass along to others—often  through e-mail (viral marketing will be discussed further in Chapter 5).
- **Community marketing:** Joining or forming a shared-interest community whose members are likely to enjoy your product or service. Note that with community marketing, it is important to place the good of the community first, and marketing efforts last.  Marketing will evolve naturally through participation.
- **Buzz marketing:** Creating an air of excitement or mystery around your business, usually through news, entertainment, or underground campaigns.
- **Grassroots marketing:** Coordinating groups of volunteers to spread your message on a personal or local level.
- **Cause marketing:** Dedicating part of your business to a social cause, which in turn earns respect and support from others dedicated to the same cause.
- **Conversion creation:** Catch phrases, promotions, launch parties, and other memorable tools or events designed to spread through word of mouth.
- **Product seeding:** Identifying influential or key individuals and getting your product or information into the right hands at the right time.

**How do you do it?**

As previously stated, even though word of mouth is effective, it's hard to pull off. If you try to fake a buzz for your business, consumers will smell a scam and your efforts will backfire.

There are, however, a few things you can do to help encourage word of mouth advertising to start on its own.

1. *Have a quality product or service.* This may sound too obvious to consider, but it is perhaps the most important factor in word of mouth marketing. Make sure your customers are getting what they pay for. Research the competition -- you're going to want to know if several other businesses are offering comparable products or services at far lower (or higher) prices than you. If possible, back your product or service with a guarantee or warrantee.

2. *Put your customers first.* A happy customer is one who feels their purchases are important to your business. Happy customers are potential word of mouth marketing sources. Make delivering on your promises a top priority. If you offer fast shipping, be certain your products are always delivered in a reliable and timely manner. If your service promises quick turnaround, make sure you never miss a deadline. Address customer complaints and problems immediately and personally, and consider offering refunds or bonuses for dissatisfied customers.

3. *Identify and speak to your target market.* Who is interested in your products or services? Where do they tend to gather -- either on or off-line? Blanket advertising is ineffective at best. Your marketing efforts should be concentrated on those venues or locations where your target consumer group is most likely to see your message. Once you create a community buzz among people whose shared interests lead them to your business, your marketing campaign becomes self-supporting.

4. *Make it easy for your customers to tell others about your business.* Word of mouth marketing is based on spreading your message. However, if interested customers don't

have a way to share their enthusiasm with others right away, they may not remember what excited them about your product or service. Provide your face-to-face customers with business cards, flyers, or an accessible sign-up list for your company newsletter (you do have a newsletter, don't you?). Online, tools such as forums and refer-a-friend programs will help to facilitate spreading the word.

5. *Listen and respond.* If you receive a single complaint, you can often deal with it on a personal, individual basis. However, if you receive several similar complaints, you may need to do more than simply reply to the dissatisfied customers. Be prepared to make changes in your business according to the wants and needs of your customers. This applies to positive suggestions as well as complaints. Also, if you discover that your business is being slammed, don't be afraid to defend yourself in a logical, reasonable manner (avoid flame wars). Customers respect businesses that are willing to admit their mistakes and will try to repair the damage.

## Summary

- Word of mouth marketing happens when a product or service "sells itself" through the enthusiasm of the consumer
- Word of mouth marketing cannot be faked; it stems from genuine compassion on the part of both business and customer
- There are many different forms word of mouth marketing can take
- Word of mouth marketing cannot be engineered, but it can be encouraged
- The customer is the most important factor in word of mouth marketing
- Word of mouth marketing is one of the least expensive and most powerful forms of Creative marketing

## *Canvassing*

You may have seen this term used in conjunction with political campaigns, and in fact that's one of the most common reasons to employ canvassing. However, this technique can also be used effectively for Creative marketing.

## What is it?

Canvassing refers to advertising that reaches out to a group of target consumers, usually in the same geographic location, on an individual level. A simple example of a canvassing campaign would be a new pizza place sending its employees out with stacks of flyers, to be left on or under as many doors in their delivery area as possible.

Other canvassing techniques include:

- Door to door introductions (think Jehovah's Witness here).
- Parking lot flyer distribution.
- Sidewalk or mall sampling.
- Telephone campaigns.

## How do you do it?

Though there is some monetary expense involved in most canvassing campaigns (usually to print the materials you plan to distribute), this type of marketing can be both inexpensive and effective. There are three stages to a successful canvassing campaign: planning, preparation, and distribution.

*Planning:* This, of course, is the most important. You have to plan the materials themselves, and you also have to determine the distribution area or method that will be most effective for you and your business.

For a local business, you will of course be interested in canvassing locally. You can distribute flyers door to door (be sure to check your area laws before you start passing out material this way), hang them on community bulletin boards or telephone poles (again, check with local ordinances here), or plan an area mailing campaign.

You can also make arrangements with other local businesses to hand out your materials (flyers, business cards, brochures, and bookmarks, to name a few) in exchange for advertising for them. If you have materials available, be sure to stay alert in regards to community events that may attract your target market.

If your business is primarily online, your canvassing area will consist of websites and forums your target customers frequent, as well as individual e-mails. Be sure to do your research and have a list of these places, along with the methods you can use to attract interest there (banner ads, forum memberships, guest blogging, articles, newsletters, and the like).

When planning your materials, make sure you spend some time getting them as attractive and interesting as possible. Comb your wording for spelling and grammatical errors -- not only can these make for a bad first impression to customers, but they can also end up with some unintended consequences. As an extreme example, imagine what would happen if the Motel Six chain missed a typo, and launched an advertising campaign for Motel Sex!

Your mistakes may not be as outrageous, but if you make a mistake in your advertising materials, your customers will be more likely to remember you for your mistakes than the quality of your products or services.

Also, make sure your material is exciting and compelling. Remember your USP? Take the aspect of your business that sets it apart from your competitors and emphasize it in your marketing copy. If you can come up with a catchy phrase or slogan, a recognizable icon, or a fun play on words that describes your business, this short and sweet message can go a long way on your materials.

*Preparation:* Once you've decided on your materials, you have to create them. If you are sending out a small batch of flyers, business cards, or brochures, you may be able to make them yourself with a high-quality printer. A commercial printer is usually more economical for larger quantities. Places like Staples and Kinko's have become more affordable than ever, and there are several competitive online companies like VistaPrint.com to choose from as well.

You will need to supply the printer with a file to print from. With the proliferation of desktop publishing software, you will likely be able to design the materials yourself. However, be sure to invest a lot of time and make it a professional presentation. If you don't feel confident in creating great-looking and sounding promotional material, you may want to consider hiring a freelance designer or copywriter -- you'll pay a one-time price for material you can use over and over.

*Distribution:* This refers to actually getting the material to your customers. You can distribute flyers yourself, or enlist volunteers to help. Volunteers, partners, or anyone who's willing to spend some time helping you promote may be willing to stand in high-traffic areas like malls or transportation terminals and hand out your material.

You may be mailing out your materials, in which case your distribution involves a trip to the post office. If you're partnering with another local business, you'll simply have to drop off a stack of materials with them.

If you plan an online canvassing campaign, it's a good idea to try and coordinate the various venues and have them hit within the same time frame. Multiple banners, ads, articles, forum posts, blog entries, and e-mails that reach your target audience more than once will help to reinforce your business in their minds, and help them remember you the next time they need your product or service.

## Summary

- Canvassing is any marketing method that reaches multiple consumers on an individual basis
- There are many forms of canvassing, including flyer and brochure distribution, sampling, telephone or door-to-door marketing, and online campaigns
- Canvassing is most effective when you have researched your target market demographic and can access a number of them in the same area
- Other businesses make excellent canvassing partners, since you can reach all of their customers without much effort
- Canvassing relies on a strong message and well-written material to achieve results
- Distribution, the final step of canvassing, can take place in person, online, or through a third party

## *The Sign Says*

Signs are everywhere. A good sign can be a great tool for your business, and in true Creative marketing style, it doesn't have to cost much.

## What is it?

A sign is any at-a-glance advertisement for your business. They range in size from matchbook covers to billboards, and can be found in a wide variety of locations. Signs are familiar to just about everyone, because there are so many of them. Unfortunately, this means people often overlook them.

## How do you do it?

If you want to use signs as part of your Creative marketing campaign, there are two important factors you need to consider: design and placement

*What it should look like*

Creating an effective sign means making it stand out from its surroundings, and giving it some individual and memorable characteristics. At the same time, you have to strike a balance between information and clutter.

You may want to consider hiring a professional designer. As with printed advertising materials, the one-time investment often proves worthwhile, since you can use the design over and over again.

However, if you feel confident that you can create your own signs, here are some tips for effective design:

- Make sure it's legible from the distance most people will view it. At the least, you will include your website and/or phone number, but if no one can read your sign, they won't contact you for more information.
- Speaking of information, don't include too much. The object of a sign is to get people interested in learning more about your business, so don't attempt to close a sale with just your sign.
- Apply the KISS principle: **K**eep **I**t **S**hort & **S**imple. Elaborate designs and excessive wording will distract rather than attract attention. Ideally, your sign should contain 3 to 10 words in addition to your contact information.
- Include a "grabber" element -- either a strong word or phrase in large text, or an intriguing image or company logo.
- Pay attention to color scheme, and make sure they are contrasting enough to stand out so everything is easily legible. Some excellent color combinations include black on white, black on yellow, white on black, yellow on black, and blue on white.

- What is not there is just as important as what is. You should incorporate approximately 30 to 40 percent of "white space" (not necessarily white, but space with no words or images on it) in the overall design of your sign.

*Where to put it*

After you design your sign, you'll need to figure out where to put it. Of course, there are the traditional places -- billboards, storefronts, bulletin boards, and the like. You can also get creative and find other places or venues for your signs.

- Restroom signs are becoming more popular. Some businesses will allow you to advertise in their bathrooms, and one creative company has actually placed advertisements inside men's urinals with some success.
- Roadside placement: Got a house on a road with decent foot or vehicle traffic? How about friends in prime locations? Try placing a sign in your front yard, and recruiting friends to do the same.
- Check with community event coordinators -- you may be able to place signs at bake sales, fundraisers, and other local happenings.
- Consider swapping signage space with other businesses in your area for greater exposure.

## Summary

- Though signs are associated with traditional advertising, they can be part of a successful Creative marketing campaign
- A sign is any at-a-glance advertisement for your business
- Design and placement are the two key elements for successful signs
- Creative sign placement can boost your signs' effectiveness

## Vehicle and Body Advertising

**This space for rent:** Attractive signs for your business are great, but they are stationary -- the only people who see them are those who walk or drive by them. In many ways, mobile signs can attract more attention.

What better way to get your signs in motion than to put them on a moving vehicle... or a moving person?

## What is it?

*Vehicle advertising:* The most obvious examples are the small signs you may have seen on city buses. Transportation companies often rent space on their fleet vehicles to advertisers as an additional source of income. This means anywhere the bus goes, your advertising will be seen by the people in the area, both foot traffic and vehicle traffic.

Other forms of vehicle advertising include:

- Interior bus signs
- Taxi and limo billboards
- Bumper stickers
- Vehicle wraps
- Self-service

*Body advertising:* How about a walking, talking advertisement for your business? You can find people who are willing, for a small fee, to wear temporary tattoos advertising your product or service. These tattoos often make a great conversation piece, and can make a lot of people aware of your business.

## How do you do it?

*Vehicle advertising:* For bus, taxi, and limo advertising, contact your local transportation companies and ask about their ad rates for fleet vehicles. You will probably need to supply your own designs for the ads, but the rates are often fairly inexpensive for the amount of exposure you'll receive. Be sure to spend a lot of time coming up with a catchy advertisement!

You can have custom bumper stickers printed for your business. It's a good idea to feature your (easy to remember) website prominently on a custom bumper sticker. Give them away to family, friends, customers, and at community events. Consider supplying free bumper stickers to other local businesses, to give away to their customers.

Vehicle wraps are partial or full vehicle advertisements that generate some interesting reactions. You pay people -- usually those who drive back and forth to work every day -- to have their personal vehicles "wrapped" with advertisements for your business.

You can also wrap your own personal vehicle, or get body or window detailing done with your business information. No matter where you drive, you will constantly be advertising your product or service!

*Body advertising:* Your first step here is to design a compelling temporary tattoo that people can identify quickly with your business. Again, it is a good idea to prominently feature your URL in the design, to allow prospective customers to find more information quickly.

When choosing people to wear your temporary tattoos:

- Decide how much you're willing to pay each person you recruit. You may want to base this on the number of days the tattoo should remain visible and in good condition.

- Specify where the tattoo should be worn. The back of the hand is a good, prominent place, though some advertisers have requested that people place them on their foreheads.
- Instruct the recruits as to what information you'd like them to give when people ask about their tattoos. You may want to consider providing them with business cards, brochures, bookmarks, or other promotional items to hand out to those who show interest.
- Ask them to keep track of how many people they talk to concerning the tattoos, so you can use the information in your marketing calculations.

**Summary**

- Vehicle and body advertising serve as mobile signs for your business
- There are many different forms of vehicle advertising, some more expensive than others
- Body advertising is enlisting other people to place advertisements for your business on a visible part of their bodies
- Vehicle and body advertisements must be eye-catching and compelling in order to attract interest
- You will need an easy-to-remember URL to incorporate prominently in your vehicle or body advertising design
- Don't forget to enlist yourself, your personal vehicle, and your own body as advertising tools for your business!

## *Promotional Items*

Everyone loves getting free stuff. Promotional items combine this basic element of human psychology with marketing flair for an effective and memorable component of a Creative advertising campaign.

**What is it?**

A "promotional item" can be any of hundreds of different things. Basically, it's any physical item that bears a printed mention of your business. Your promotional items can be traditional or unique. You can give them away free, award them to customers for buying certain things or participating in special offers, and even sell them (if they are high quality and in demand) as an additional source of income.

Following is a list of a few traditional and not-so-traditional promotional items that can be customized for your business:

- Brochures and sales catalogues
- Bookmarks
- Printed newsletters
- Glossy flyers
- Business cards
- Magnets
- Bumper stickers
- Key chains
- Coffee mugs
- Shot glasses
- Water goblets
- Tee shirts
- Sweatshirts
- Baseball caps
- Sweatbands
- Bandannas
- Stress balls
- Stuffed animals
- Coasters

- Posters
- Matchbooks
- Lanyards
- Napkins
- Toothpick holders
- Pens/pencils
- Calendars
- Tote bags
- Travel clocks
- Travel mirrors
- Combs/brushes
- Box cutters
- Towels/washcloths

## How do you do it?

Effective promotional products are intriguing, fitting, and carry just enough information without overburdening your customers. Here are some tips on creating effective promotional items:

*Design with signs in mind.* Keep the information on promotional products simple and to the point -- include your business name, slogan, and contact information (phone number and/or website). After all, if the item is slathered with text, no one is going to want to actually use it.

*Choose items that reflect your business.* If you run a catering company, custom napkins and other kitchen items are good choices; whereas combs, brushes, and towels might not be such a good fit. However, just about any promotional item can be adapted to any business with a little creativity.

*Make your items fun and attractive.* Bookmarks are great, but how many people do you know that actually use them? Unless your main product is a printed book, if you have a bunch of bookmarks made they will probably end up in the trash. Consider what your customers like to do, and base your promotional item decision on your best guess at what will interest them. Custom puzzles, anyone?

*Shop around for the best deals.* Unless you're creating your promotional items yourself (and it is certainly possible, though time-consuming), you will likely look for a custom printer or manufacturer to emblazon your message on hundreds of items. There are dozens of great places online, including Café Press ([www.cafepress.com](www.cafepress.com)), which lets you create and purchase your own items at cost, with bulk discounts for larger orders. You might also want to purchase bulk novelty items from a company like the Oriental Trading Company ([www.orientaltrading.com](www.orientaltrading.com)) and modify the items yourself.

*Distribute your items freely and often.* Always keep several promotional items with you, and hand them out constantly. You never know when you'll meet someone who will later become your customer -- and you will at the very least make a bunch of folks happy by giving them free stuff! Don't forget the power of giveaways in conjunction with your main business. Offer to give your promotional items to customers with every purchase. Post the freebie notice in your physical location or on your website, as well as message boards and freebie forums for more exposure.

## Summary

- A promotional item is any physical, tangible item that bears a message or advertisement for your business
- There are hundreds of promotional items to choose from
- You can make just about anything into a promotional item
- Promotional items should relate to your business in some way
- Effective promotional items bear simple messages and contact information
- The best promotional items are fun or useful for your customers

- You should always keep a supply of promotional items on hand

# Chapter 4 – Digital Creative Marketing

Whether your business is a traditional store, a work-from-home operation, or a completely online venture, a strong web presence is a must in today's fast-paced marketing world. In the age of instant information, businesses without websites have a decided disadvantage.

One of the most important things to keep in mind when it comes to online marketing is that despite the instantaneous nature of the Internet, there are no overnight success methods. Just like a live marketing campaign, your online Creative marketing efforts will require time and effort in order to succeed.

In this chapter, we'll discuss the ins and outs of online promotion, and learn some Creative marketing techniques you can use to further your business on the Internet, whether or not it's based online.

## *Establishing yourself*

If you want customers, you need to make people aware of your website. You also have to make sure your website is a good place to be. Your basic goals with online marketing are to generate traffic to your website, and to keep visitors there when they arrive (and keep them coming back).

We'll talk about this in reverse order, since you need your website up and running before you start attracting visitors.

### Website basics

A website can be a very powerful marketing tool. However, a bad website can have a powerful but opposing effect: driving off not only current visitors, but also everyone they know, when they start telling everyone on the 'net how terrible your website looks, or how difficult it is to navigate.

Keep in mind that there are millions of websites out there, and if yours does not attract a visitor's attention with their first look, they'll simply go to the next page of search results and give their business to someone else.

Does your website pass the first-look test? Here are some rules to keep in mind:

- Your URL, or website address (www.YourWebSite.com) should be easy to remember and spell, and contain very few, if any, special characters or alternate spellings. This not only looks more professional when visitors find a link to your website online, but it also makes it much easier to translate real-world advertisements into website visitors. You should include your URL on all of your physical marketing material.

- Your home page should be visually pleasing, easy to read, and not cluttered with text. Make sure all of your important information is contained in the top portion of your home page (the area visible on a screen when a visitor first arrives at the site) -- but *do not* try to cram everything on the home page. Include links to essential pages rather than lengthy descriptions of everything.

- Flash animation is great, but a huge flash presentation on your home page not only slows down your load time (to the point where visitors will not bother waiting for the page to display), but also turns off many casual Internet users. If you must use Flash animation, keep it to a minimum and don't use it to convey essential information.

- If you have a newsletter, include an e-mail link or a subscription box on every page of your website. The more visible your options are, the greater the chances people will find them.

- Your website should be an informative place. A hard-sell website ("This product/service is amazing! Buy it now!") does not appeal to most Web browsers. Be sure to post news and current events concerning your business, and consider providing informative articles that educate visitors on topics pertaining to your products or services.

- Update often. Keeping your content fresh not only makes search engines happy, it also provides visitors with a reason to keep coming back!

- Make your content keyword-rich without being blatant. Brainstorm a list of search terms Internet users might type into a search engine when looking for a website like yours, and use each of those terms a few times. Do not clump together lists of keywords; instead, sprinkle them throughout your content. The practice of keyword stuffing can get your website banned from search engines.

- Be user-friendly! Test your website using several different screen resolutions to make sure the text and images are not too crowded or spread out. Check your links and navigation controls frequently -- few things are more frustrating to an Internet user than dead or outdated links. Make sure every page includes a link to your home page and a link to your sales or "landing" page, at the very least.

## Internet marketing basics

Just about all "traditional" forms of Internet marketing can be classified as Creative marketing. This is because Internet advertising is generally inexpensive or free, involves an investment of your time and effort, and must be presented in a unique manner if you want to stand out from the millions of other websites competing for attention.

It is a good idea to incorporate basic Internet marketing into your Creative campaign. If you have never promoted a website before, you may not be familiar with the basic concepts of spreading the e-word. Here are a few ideas to get you started (remember, all these tactics should be implemented *after* your website is optimized, fine-tuned, double-checked and ready for business):

- The more search engines your website is listed on, the greater the chance customers will stumble across it. The "big" search engines such as Google and

Yahoo! do not allow manual submissions, but your website will automatically be picked up within a few weeks by their web trawlers. However, smaller search engines like AltaVista, Dogpile, and ExactSeek may not automatically include your site. There are many free search engine submission programs online that will submit your website to multiple engines for inclusion. Be sure to have a list of keywords and a brief (two to three sentences) description of your website available while you're submitting.

- If you have a newsletter, you can list your website in multiple newsletter or e-zine directories in the same way you submit to search engine. Having a free, regular newsletter or e-zine that contains interesting and informative material is a great way to build customer loyalty and attract new business online. Your subscribers will be more likely to purchase your products or services, since they will see your business multiple times.

- Banner ad exchange programs are another possibility for Internet exposure. When you design your banner ad, keep in mind the rules for creating an effective sign and apply them to the banner. If you don't have any computer experience, there are several programs that will allow you to generate a banner ad using their template for free. Then, seek similar or complementary websites to your business and offer to host their banner in exchange for hosting theirs on your website.

- Pay-per-click (PPC) advertising is effective in many cases, and though it does require a monetary investment, the amount is small (usually 2 to 5 cents per visitor). One example of a good pay-per-click program is Google AdWords (http://adwords.google.com) -- the program does not require minimum monthly spending, and the average bidding rate for lesser search terms is 2 to 3 cents. Google also includes a keyword generator to help you write more effective ads. More information is available through the preceding link.

### *Going Viral*

Viral marketing is one of the most powerful forms of Internet advertising available. It takes basic online marketing a step further: basically, you get the ball rolling, and hundreds of other Internet users pick it up and run with it.

## What is it?

Viral marketing is more or less the Internet term for word-of-mouth. The term "viral marketing" refers to any advertising method that encourages people who receive a message to pass it on to others.

One classic example of a viral marketing strategy was demonstrated by Microsoft Networks Hotmail program. Hotmail was one of the first free web-based e-mail providers. In order to let people know about the program, Microsoft included a tag or signature at the bottom of every outgoing e-mail their customers sent, reading: "Get your private, free e-mail at http://www.hotmail.com", that was linked to Hotmail's main page. People receiving messages from users with Hotmail accounts set up their own, and then e-mailed more people with the same tag on every message. The number of Hotmail users ballooned in no time.

In essence, Microsoft invented the e-mail signature, another powerful marketing tool now used by millions online.

Keep in mind that viral marketing does not simply spread your message from person to person. Effective viral marketing spreads from person to people, making your advertising program an exponential success.

## How do you do it?

The best way to engage in viral marketing online is to make it easy for your customers to spread your message. There are quite a few ways to do this:

- *Newsletters or e-zines:* Since most newsletters and e-zines are delivered via e-mail, it's easy for your customers to hit forward and pass them on to several friends. However, this will only happen if you include good, quality information in your electronic publication. Rather than simply advertising your products or services, consider writing articles, hosting guest columns, and generally providing your customers with something fun.

- *Article syndication:* Once you have written articles for your newsletter or e-zine, share the knowledge by uploading them to article syndication websites. These are "article banks" used by web masters looking for fresh content for their own websites. Essentially, you are giving anyone permission to reprint your article, with the caveat that your authorship and a link to your website is included. Article syndication creates inbound links that boost your website's search engine rank, and make it more likely customers will find you.

- *Refer-a-friend programs:* Got something valuable to give your customers, such as bonus products or promotional items? Consider using a refer-a-friend program: in exchange for providing you with a number of e-mail addresses to which you can send a one-time announcement about your business, you can give your customers something they'll enjoy, and make them eager to tell their friends about your website.

- *Link-swapping and banner placement:* As mentioned in the previous section, the more links there are on the Internet leading to your website, the greater your exposure will be. Offer to host other websites' links and banner ads on your site in exchange for a reciprocal link from theirs. Also, keep in mind that inbound links (links that point to your website, and are not linked back from your website) carry more weight with search engines than outbound or reciprocal links. Try to post as many inbound links as you can.

- *Giveaways, contests, and freebies:* Once again, everyone loves to get something for nothing. Sponsoring contests and giveaways will naturally generate the urge for your customers to tell others about your website, so everyone they know can get the free deal or enter the contest. Don't hesitate to give away the occasional product or service in exchange for the marketing value it can bring your business!

- *Online communities and forums:* Joining forums and communities dedicated to topics that will interest your customers is a great way to get your name out there. Remember, online etiquette dictates that you do not simply join a forum and immediately post advertisements. Spend some time getting to know other forum members, and they will be happy to tell others in the community about you and your business.

As with other forms of advertising, your message has to be compelling and interesting, or no one will want to pass it on. Make sure to spend as much time developing your advertising message as you do spreading it around. Don't forget to include your USP, any promotions or freebies you may be running, and your website and contact information.

**Summary**

- Viral marketing is the Internet form of word-of-mouth
- The keys to viral marketing are to create a compelling message and make it easy for people to pass it on
- Viral marketing represents an exponential increase in online exposure for your business
- There are several different viral marketing methods you can take advantage of for your website
- Viral marketing messages must be interesting, informative, or valuable in order to be successfully spread

## *Beating the Blog Drum*

Do you blog? Even if you don't, chances are you have already seen several blogs online, though you might not be aware of this relatively new website format. Blogs create a sense of community and provide an outlet for many different types of information, both business and personal.

## What is it?

Blog, short for web log, is a specialized type of website that acts like an electronic journal. Blog users can type in text, upload pictures and sound, and instantly post it to the site. Blog software formats each entry in the blog style you select, automatically creates entry archives and permanent links to each page, and allows for easy customization.

Most blogs also allow comments from visitors. There are comment screening options you can use to disallow anonymous comments, comments from non-bloggers, or comments altogether. However, the comments feature is one of the most powerful components of a blog, because visitors can enjoy instant interaction with you.

Blogs allow you to speak with your customers on a personal level. Once Internet users get to know the person behind the business, they will be more likely to purchase your products or services. Trust is a valuable commodity online, and blogs help you build up a trust bank.

Best of all, most blogs are free to create and use, so you won't have to spend a penny on your blog.

A few of the most popular blog providers are:

Blogger -- www.blogger.com: Owned by Google. Fully featured free blogs with customizable templates, easy to use

LiveJournal - www.livejournal.com: Similar to Blogger, offers paid upgrades for additional special features

WordPress - www.wordpress.com: Another popular free blogger platform with millions of users, easy interfaces and lots of template choices

Blogs have become so popular, there are millions of bloggers (people with blogs) online communicating tons of information, opinions, and chats every day. In fact, the blog collective on the Internet has become powerful enough to merit its own term: the blogosphere. The blogosphere as a whole is extremely influential, and often when one blog carries an item of interest, others will pick it up and spread it across the Internet.

## How do you do it?

Using a blog for business purposes is a twofold process. First, you have to build a readership for your blog. Then, you can enlist other bloggers to help you get more exposure for yours.

*Building a readership*

Like your website, you should plan to keep your blog informative and entertaining, and update regularly. Many bloggers post to their blogs daily, and often include links to other websites with news or information they believe may interest their readers. It is a good idea to choose a posting schedule (daily, Monday through Friday, bi-weekly, weekly -- whatever you're comfortable keeping up with) and stick to it.

The single most effective way to gain readers for your blog is to visit other people's blogs and leave thoughtful comments on their posts. Do not simply comment that you have a blog and you want them to visit; this is viewed as spam, or at the very least, rude.

Of course, contacting individual bloggers is a time-consuming process. Another way to attract readers is to list your blog in as many blog directories as you can find. This way, Internet users will be able to find your blog through search engines.

Post a link to your blog on your website, and include one in your e-mail signature. The more people know about your blog, the more likely you will be to get visitors.

*Working in the blogosphere*

Other bloggers are an excellent marketing resource. Most blogging software includes an easy tool to add links to your sidebar. You can link to several other blogs that may be of interest to your readers -- and in most cases, the bloggers you link to will automatically link back to your blog, since this is considered common courtesy. Some bloggers will list an e-mail address you can contact them through to exchange blog links. Take advantage of these when you find them.

You can also participate in guest blogging -- writing an entry for someone else's blog for a day. Since bloggers always need fresh content, many are happy to host other people's articles as long as they pertain to their readers. Find blogs that are similar to yours and request to be a guest blogger. Remember to include a link to your website at the end of your post!

## Summary

- Blogs are a specialized form of website that act like online journals
- The millions of blogs online are collectively known as the blogosphere
- Bloggers (people who blog) and blog readers are very influential online
- Most blogs are free to set up, and have easy templates that don't require HTML coding knowledge
- Like your website, your blog should be informative, entertaining, and updated regularly

- Visit other people's blogs and link to them to get increased traffic for your blog

- Becoming a guest blogger is a great way to get more exposure for your business

# Chapter 5 – Rules and Regulations

Following the rules is an important step in Creative marketing. Some people view Creative marketing tactics as too aggressive, and many a marketer has been threatened with legal action.

However, if you're familiar with what you can and cannot do, you will not have to worry about this. Make sure you protect yourself!

## *Fairness in Advertising*

Honesty is still the best policy. Consumers don't appreciate being lied to, and nothing spreads faster -- both online and in your community -- than news of a dishonest business.

Therefore, it's important that you practice fairness in advertising.

### What It Means

Fairness in advertising is really a simple concept: don't claim your product or service does something that it doesn't. For example, a diet pill company claiming their product will "make you lose 50 pounds overnight!" is clearly mistaken -- this is a physical impossibility, unless you amputate your legs. Even with a quantifier like "practically" or "almost" (You'll lose 50 pounds practically overnight!), the statement remains implausible. Every person's idea of "practically" is different.

What would be fair for our fictitious diet pill company to claim? It depends on what the product actually does. In this scenario, the company may be able to state that their diet pill helps you lose weight "faster than the leading brands" or even that you may notice *results* "practically overnight" (not 50 pounds worth of results, of course!).

Your wording is essential when practicing fairness in advertising. You can get creative, but there is a fine line between creativity and false claims. In most cases, it's best to let your product or service speak for itself.

Customer testimonials are an excellent way to incorporate fairness in advertising. Getting real statements from the people who have used your product or service not only keeps you honest, but also allows consumers to trust you more, because the opinions are coming from someone who has no vested interest in your business.

Don't lie to your customers, and they will thank you with their business.

## Spam Isn't Healthy

One of the most pervasive myths in online advertising today is this: the more people you e-mail, the more money you'll make. But if you're using bulk e-mail to get there, you're on the wrong track.

No one likes spam. In the Internet world, the term "spam" refers to any e-mail advertising a product or service that you did not ask to receive (and not the lunchmeat-in-a-can pictured above). There are a lot of marketing "gurus" who insist that sending cold bulk e-mails still gets results -- and that may have been true when the Internet was still in its infancy, but today's online community is more perceptive than ever, and it's almost impossible to slip by the collective spam radar.

If you look, you can find several hundred places that will sell you lists of thousands of e-mail addresses for a few dollars. The temptation to buy these lists is strong... who can resist thousands of potential customers in one shot, without the many hours of research it takes to build a solid opt-in list of your own?

You can! Here's why you should:

- Spamming alienates potential customers. When people receive spam, often their first reaction is to delete it unread, and most will block all further communication from that particular e-mail address: yours.
- Many Internet users hate spam so much, they will take action to shut you down. This can range from reporting you to your ISP (Internet service provider), to flaming (sending hate mail) or "mail bombs" (sending hundreds or thousands of files with very large attachments designed to crash your server).
- Your business can be blacklisted. There is an actual Internet advertiser's blacklist that warns consumers about spammers, and you don't want to be connected with that list.
- Spamming just plain doesn't work! There are so many dangerous scams online today that most Internet users are reluctant to even open any unsolicited messages. Even if you write the most brilliant and enticing advertising message in the world, if you send it through bulk e-mail, no one will ever read it.

In short: don't spam. Do the work and create your own list of people who actually want to hear what you have to say. Your business will benefit enormously, and you won't be branded as a charlatan.

### *Weird Laws and Ordinances*

As a Creative marketer, it's important for you to obey the law. If a customer feels you are trying to con them, skirt legal issues, or harass them into buying your product or service, you could end up with a lot more trouble than a lost sale.

You can familiarize yourself with basic marketing dos and don'ts through the Federal Trade Commission (FTC), the government organization that regulates and protects consumers in the United States. Browse their website at www.ftc.gov for more information on advertising guidance, antitrust laws, and FTC procedures regarding consumer complaints.

You should also check with your local Chamber of Commerce, and request information on advertising laws that affect your business. Find the nearest Chamber to you here: http://www.uschamber.com/chambers/directory/default

Does your city or state have strange laws that forbid a certain Creative marketing method? The website Dumb Laws (www.dumblaws.com) provides a collection of weird, outrageous and outlandish laws that are still on the books. Here is a sampling of some laws that might hinder your marketing efforts:

- In **Alabama**, it is illegal to impersonate a person of the clergy -- so don't dress up as a priest to promote your business.
- You can be fined $25 for flirting in **New York**. Beware of approaching strangers!
- Speaking of truth in advertising, a jail term of up to one year awaits you in **Louisiana** for making a false promise.
- Watch out, mobile billboard advertisers in **Ohio**: the Ohio driver's education manual states that you must honk the horn when you pass another vehicle.
- In **Texas**, it is illegal to sell one's eye. Keep your body parts close at hand.
- **Florida** forbids "unnatural acts" with another person... so forget playing Twister on the sidewalk. Also, it's illegal to skateboard without a license.
- Unless you own at least two cows, you may not wear cowboy boots in **California**.
- Seasonal business owners should note that in **Maine**, you will be fined for displaying Christmas decorations after January 14.
- Your profits will come in handy in **Illinois**, where you can be arrested for vagrancy if you don't have at least one dollar on your person.

What strange laws does your state have? Perhaps one of them will give you an idea for your Creative marketing campaign!

# Chapter 6 – Welcome to the Jungle

Are you ready to become a Creative?

Without a doubt, Creative marketing is an extremely effective strategy for any small business. Since you typically will not have a huge advertising budget, it makes more sense to invest effort and time, and reap the rewards of your careful planning and creativity.

Some points to remember:

- You will get out of your Creative marketing campaign what you put into it. If you do not invest the effort, you will not reap the rewards.
- A successful Creative marketing campaign is ongoing, and consists of more than one strategy or tactic.
- Be patient: Creative success will not come to you overnight, but it will come!
- Think outside the box (in fact, try to come up with your own term for thinking outside the box as an exercise in creativity). The unique aspects of your business will generate better profits when you leverage them.
- Do not view other businesses as your competition. Instead, view them as potential partners and cultivate mutually beneficial relationships.
- Never pass up an opportunity to market (but keep it casual where it's appropriate to refrain from being pushy).
- Be prepared to watch your business leap forward!

Creative marketing is not just a strategy... it's a state of mind. When you learn to think like a Creative, you will greatly improve your business marketing skills -- not to mention your profits.

www.ingramcontent.com/pod-product-compliance
Lightning Source LLC
LaVergne TN
LVHW021305200726
843509LV00012B/1796